■SCHOLASTIC

‖‖‖‖‖‖‖‖‖
W9-CRE-567

# Let's Find Out™

# Let's Play a Five Senses Guessing Game

## Amanda Miller · Joan Michael

Scholastic Inc.
New York  Toronto  London  Auckland  Sydney
Mexico City  New Delhi  Hong Kong  Buenos Aires

**Literacy Specialist:** Francie Alexander, Chief Academic Officer, Scholastic Inc.
**Art Director:** Joan Michael

**Photographs:** James Levin (gold coins, dirty socks, colored duct tape, all photos of boy);
©William A. Bolton/Alamy (fall foliage detail); ©Bob Elsdale/Getty Images (rabbit);
©Canopy Photography/Veer (mouse); ©Darrin Klimek/Getty Images (towels); ©Digital
Vision/Getty (Sharpei); ©Fancy Photography/Veer (fall foliage); ©Food Collection/Getty
Images (lemons); ©GK Hart/Vikki Hart/Getty Images (frog); ©Iconica/Getty Images
(pie); ©Image Source (perfume bottle); ©Photodisc (watermelon, pepper, pinecone);
©Photodisc/Veer (macaw, jingle bells, pretzel); ©Photonica/Getty (crying baby);
©Stockdisc/Getty Images (tiara)

ISBN 0-439-91575-9

2 3 4 5 6 7 8 9 10     40     18 17 16 15 14

I use my five senses every day. So do you!
Let's play a five senses guessing game.

I see with my eyes.
I look at the world around me.
There's so much to see every day.

# Here is what I saw today.

shiny coins

a sparkly tiara

a colorful bird

a wrinkled dog

I hear with my ears.
I listen carefully to hear soft sounds.
I cover my ears when sounds are too loud!

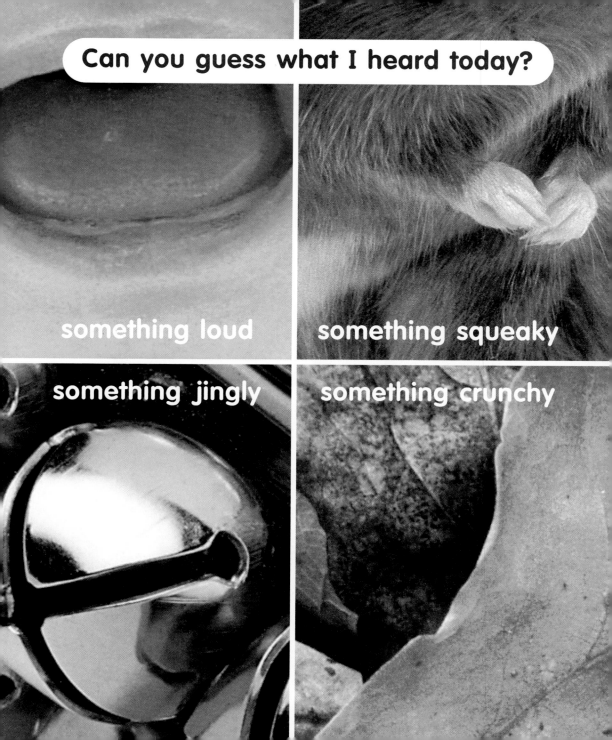

# Here is what I heard today.

a squeaky mouse

a loud baby

crunchy leaves

jingly bells

**Stop** that loud crying!!!!!

what did you **hear** today?
How did it **Sound**?

I smell with my nose.
Sniff, sniff! Some things smell good
and some things don't!

Can you guess what I smelled today?

something stinky

something flowery

something fresh

something sweet

# Here is what I smelled today.

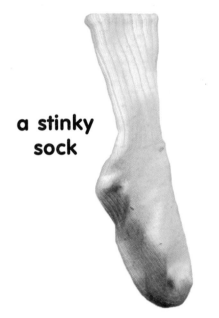

a stinky sock

flowery perfume

fresh towels

a sweet pie

EEWWW! Stinky!
what did you smell today?
How did it smell?

I **taste** with my tongue. I like to try new foods. There are lots of wonderful things to taste!

# Here is what I tasted today.

a sweet watermelon

a sour lemon

a spicy pepper

a salty pretzel

what did you **taste** today?
How did it **taste**?

Yum! So Sweet!

I touch things with my fingers to learn how they feel. I also feel with my skin. A cool breeze feels good on my face and arms.

# Sometimes, I use all my senses together. That's why I love popcorn!

How does it look? Fluffy!
How does it sound? Crunchy!
How does it smell? Buttery!
How does it taste? Salty!
How does it feel? Bumpy!
How did you use all your senses today?